North Yorkshire Railway S

by Norman Ellis

STAINTON DALE STATION

Stainton Dale Station was on the Scarborough & Whitby Railway and, as with Scalby and Cloughton Stations (which it resembled), opened in 1885 and closed in 1965. The stationmaster is about to pass the tablet in his right hand to the driver of a southbound train, thus giving priority over the next stretch of single track.

NORTH EASTERN RAILWAY.

ATTRACTIONS IN HARROGATE:
Grand Opera House—Stephen Pritts' Repertoire Co.

Passengers will be admitted at the EARLY DOORS of the Grand Opera House, Harrogate, without extra payment, on production of the return halves of their Excursion tickets.

ATTRACTIONS IN BRADFORD:

| Theatre Royal. | Princes Theatre. |
| "The Speckled Band." | "Daughter of the Sea." |

On Saturday, 5th November, 1910,

An Excursion train will be run as under, to

HARROGATE,
Otley and Bradford.

			Fares there and back, Third Class.		
		P.M.	To Harrogate.	To Otley.	To Bradford.
PATELEY BRIDGE		dep. 1 15			
DACRE		„ 1 23	1s	1/3	
DARLEY		„ 1 27			
BIRSTWITH		„ 1 33		1/-	
RIPLEY VALLEY		„ 1 39			
MASHAM		„ 1 8	1s 3d	1/6	1/9
TANFIELD		„ 1 16			
MELMERBY		„ 1 24	1s	1/3	
RIPON		„ 1 46			
WORMALD GREEN		„ 1 56			
NIDD BRIDGE		„ 2 2		1/-	
HARROGATE		„ 2 20			
PANNAL		„ 2 25			1/6
WEETON		„ 2 30			
OTLEY		„ 2 45			1/3

Passengers change at Harrogate in going only. Passengers change at Harrogate in each direction.

Return Arrangements the same day as follow :—

BRADFORD (Midland)	dep. 10 55 p.m.
OTLEY	„ 11 20 „
HARROGATE (for stations Ripley Valley to Pateley Bridge, except Hampsthwaite, inclusive)	„ 11 50 „
„ (for stations Nidd Bridge to Masham inclusive)	„ 12 0 mid.

Children not exceeding 3 years of age, free ; above 3 and under 12 years of age, half-fare.

The tickets issued at the above fares are only available for the excursion train to and from and to the stations at and for which they are issued, and are not transferable, and no passenger will be allowed to leave or join the train at any intermediate station. Passengers travelling by this train without having first obtained a ticket for it, will be required to pay the ordinary single fare.

The tickets are only available for those excursionists who travel by the excursion train on both outward and return journeys. Any person using the excursion train for the outward journey only, or for the return journey only, will be required to pay the ordinary fare for the journey taken, notwithstanding that such person is provided with an excursion ticket.

A limited number of carriages will be provided for this excursion, and intending passengers should apply early for tickets, which can now be obtained at the above-mentioned stations.

This excursion is advertised and arranged by the Company subject to the general conditions and regulations specified in the current time table, to which intending excursionists are referred.

NO LUGGAGE ALLOWED.

Bicycles, Perambulators and Mail Carts will be conveyed at the rate shewn in the Company's Time Table

For further information apply to Mr. W. R. RODEN, District Passenger Agent, York (Tel. No. 185a).

851   Ben Johnson & Co., Printers, York.

INTRODUCTION

Rise and Decline

Sentimentality, scenic splendour or a sense of history were not enough to prevent the closure of sizeable parts of North Yorkshire's comprehensive railway system. Why did railways, which were originally envisaged as aids to industry, so permeate this area of outstanding beauty?

In North Yorkshire, farming and fishing easily overshadowed both heavy industry and manufacturing. The agrarian ambience was evident in many of the inland market towns as well as in the villages. Holidaymakers flocked to coastal resorts and beauty spots, but only for three months of the year or at weekends. Where was the railway potential?

In the 19th Century, most roads, particularly country ones, and whatever vehicles traversed them were inadequate. Then came the newfangled railway. It was comparatively quick, smooth running, had high capacity, was a bit dirty but powerfully impressive. In the mid 1840s, railway schemes were mooted, companies were formed, Acts were passed and lines were laid. It was called railway mania. Competition was rife. If one company didn't build a line, then another soon would.

Although the first railways in North Yorkshire were constructed by several different companies, most were absorbed by the mighty North Eastern Railway, which completed the system. The exception was on the western fringe where the similarly mighty Midland Railway was all powerful.

As the 20th Century progressed, the railway network looked increasingly vulnerable. Roads and road transport had improved. Buses went into the villages, whereas many railway stations, having been built on relatively straight lines, stood a mile or more from them. The private car sounded the death knell.

The Railway Companies

The North Eastern Railway (NER) was formed in 1854 by an amalgamation of three principal railway companies which were the York, Newcastle & Berwick, the York & North Midland and the Leeds Northern. Taking into consideration past and future mergers, around fifty railways became part of the NER, including the Stockton & Darlington, which opened in 1825. The Midland Railway (MR) was formed in 1844 by an amalgamation of the North Midland, Midland Counties and the Birmingham & Derby Junction Railways. From January 1923 onwards, the NER and MR became part of the London & North Eastern (LNER) and London, Midland & Scottish Railway (LMS) Companies respectively. Railway nationalisation took effect from January 1948.

The NER dominated the counties of Northumberland and Durham as well as the North and East Ridings of Yorkshire to the almost total exclusion of all other railways. Its freight activities in Northumberland, Durham and around Middlesbrough were aimed at the coal and iron industries. However, its endeavours in North Yorkshire were originally directed mainly towards agriculture and stone. When the subsidiary potential for carrying passengers became obvious, there were no archetypal forms for stations, but only prerequisites. From these, patterns and designs began to emerge for both small and large stations. Stations differed more in configuration than in facilities offered.

Station Architecture and Architects

Sturdy, rather than extravagant, stations were the norm for both the NER and MR, but plenty of exceptions existed. At first, many smaller stations acquired a building which resembled a squarish house. With the addition of other buildings and perhaps an awning, the house element became less pronounced. For medium and larger sized stations, the North Eastern was inclined towards overall roofs, sometimes called trainsheds.

Within both the NER and MR, some uniformity of station designs might have been expected but, because each company absorbed so many different concerns or built lines over a period, only a modicum of standardisation is evident. The buildings were constructed in a variety of materials depending not only on their availability, but also financial restraints or environmental considerations. The favoured building materials were stone, brick or timber or a combination of all three. Being built to last, some early stone and brick stations have survived, though not necessarily being used for their intended purpose.

The original constituent companies of the NER commissioned architects to design their station buildings, the most notable of these being George Townsend Andrews of York. He designed stations for George Hudson, the 'Railway King', and his York & North Midland Railway. Andrews was responsible, among others, for the stations at Scarborough, Malton, Richmond, Tadcaster, Ruswarp, Sleights, Castle Howard and Spofforth.

From its formation in 1854, the NER employed its own architects. The first, Thomas Prosser (1854-74) was responsible for the original design of the second York Station. Benjamin Burleigh and William Peachey, who followed him in quick succession, were responsible for its completion in 1877.

Station Facilities and Paraphernalia

Country stations on main or branch lines usually had two platforms, although, at a few branch stations, a single platform sufficed. The stationmaster's house, an office, booking hall, waiting rooms and toilets were usually located in a set of buildings on one platform, with the opposite platform only having a waiting shed. Occasionally, instead of two platforms, a station had a twin-sided island platform with similar facilities. Platforms were connected by a ramp, footbridge or subway. Adjacent to the platforms, there was usually a level crossing for road vehicles, or alternatively a road overbridge. A signal box was frequently located on or near one of the platforms. Bay windows on the station office or waiting room were functional as well as attractive, being intended as platform lookouts.

Although less obvious, most country stations also had a goods yard, which had a warehouse, loading dock, coal cells and a crane. Large goods trains trundling through stations were a reminder of largely hidden activities at pits and quarries.

Town, city and suburban stations possessed all of the facilities of country stations, sometimes repeated on several platforms. Administrative offices, bookshops and refreshment rooms were additional features. Sometimes a concourse behind the station facade added a touch of luxury, while glazed overall roofs were common at many of the larger stations. Ticket barriers at larger stations were a 20th Century innovation. Tickets used to be collected just outside the stations at special wooden platforms where ticket collectors could walk.

The NER introduced a standardised design for its smaller platform seats as well as for its lamps. The seats consisted of two wooden planks set on cast iron legs, which were made to look like tree branches. Simple timber posts (later concrete) were used as lamp standards. In 1895, the Company launched its Best Kept Wayside Gardens competition, which led to some delightful horticultural achievements by station staff.

Weighing machines, red-painted chocolate machines and other slot machines appeared on many platforms, although the smallest stations were often denied these luxuries. Barrows in all shapes and sizes could be seen on most platforms. Milk churns, pigeon baskets, portmanteaux and metal trunks often signalled the imminent arrival of a train.

Platform clocks on wayside stations sometimes had two faces, one giving the time on the platform and the other in an inner office. Waiting rooms, with their horsehair seats and, possibly, a hefty table, were kept warm with an inviting coal fire. Signs in and around the station ranged from the simplest, which directed people to the various facilities, to detailed timetable or excursion notices. As colour printing improved, pictorial posters were used to great effect.

The Staff

At the turn of the century, almost every station had a stationmaster, which accounted for the need for a station house for him and his family. Later, when economies became necessary, some stationmasters were put in charge of two or three stations.

It was essential for porters at country stations to be jacks of all trades including filling sacks with grain or potatoes in the goods yard, cleaning windows or washing toilets. At larger stations, work tended to be more specialised. At these, there were all kinds of inspectors, clerks and the inevitable porters who always knew from which part of a train the most affluent would alight.

Random and Rambling Railway Remarks

Extracts from the epistles of Harold Smith are included in this book. He lived at 44, Hanover Square, Bradford and was employed in the printing trade. Harold had a keen interest in railways and recorded his travels in a series of hand-written illustrated booklets called *Random and Rambling Railway Remarks*. Each one was sent to a Mr Dawson, who corresponded regularly with Smith. They all capture the atmosphere of Edwardian rail travel.

Scope of this Book

Most of the illustrations, many of them previously unpublished in book form, are taken from photographs which appeared on Edwardian postcards. The area covered is that which was constituted as North Yorkshire in 1974. It excludes the parts of Cleveland which were in the North Riding, but includes northern sections of the West Riding which were seconded to North Yorkshire.

York to Scarborough

The splendid city of York, with its magnificent Minster, is a long established railway centre. The railway arrived in 1839 and parts of the 1841 York & North Midland Station still remain. The Y&NM was formed at a meeting held in York Guildhall in 1835 . George Hudson, who lived at 44, Micklegate, and George Stephenson were appointed Chairman and Engineer respectively. York has been the headquarters of the Y&NM, NER, LNER, and North Eastern and Eastern Regions of BR. The history of railways can still be relived at the National Railway Museum.

The Y&NM opened its line from York to Scarborough in 1845. Much of the architecture was by GT Andrews, including the stations at Haxby, Castle Howard, Malton and Scarborough. Most of the stations were closed to passengers in 1930, but retained goods facilities for some years after.

Scarborough was connected to Hull, via Seamer, by a series of lines which opened during 1846-7. In 1882, the NER opened a branch between Seamer and Pickering. Known as the Forge Valley Line, it was constructed almost parallel with parts of the York-Scarborough line. Its stations, being inconveniently sited, suffered badly from bus and lorry competition.

Photographed circa 1914, this view shows the North Eastern Railway's 1877 York Station as designed by Thomas Prosser. It replaced the 1841 York & North Midland Railway station which was just inside the city walls. The restrained portico on Station Road housed the road vehicle area and main entrance.

A 1920s picture with the station portico on the left and Peachey's Royal Station Hotel beyond. The hotel was opened in 1878 and subsequently enlarged in 1896. York's electric trams, which operated from 1910 to 1935 and replaced earlier horse drawn trams, were not a serious threat to local railways.

This view from the 1900 footbridge shows summer Saturday holiday crowds in 1977. In contrast to the exterior, the interior was made strikingly impressive. The great roof spans, with end screens, were supported on decorative columns and the curved site afforded a demonstration in perspective. Overall, the station has changed little since construction, but was extended westward in 1938.

Haxby Station was opened by the Y&NM in 1845 and closed by the LNER in 1930. The main station building, which incorporated the stationmaster's house, faced the road and was at right angles to the track. The signal box and level crossing are discernible near the train while the goods yard is on the left. This view dates from about 1912.

With the aristocracy at the mansion of Castle Howard in mind, a unique design was produced for the Y&NM's Castle Howard Station. In cream coloured stone, the main station building looked like a glorified gatehouse, with its curious chimneys, arched doors and windows as well as the balcony on ogee brackets overlooking the platform. Coaches conveyed the elite the $2^{1}/_{2}$ miles between the station and the mansion. The garden was an eye-catching feature at the station. This 1845 station closed to passengers in 1930 but remained open for goods for some time afterwards.

Andrews' original structure at Malton (dating from 1845) had to undergo several changes. The platform shown above was originally narrower and allowed a pair of tracks to pass under the overall roof. One set of tracks was relocated outside the station building and given its own canopy as shown on the extreme left. The barrows and personnel suggest a busy station and, as such, an ideal spot for all of those adverts on the right. Flour, ale and manure were handled in the goods yard. Malton Station is south of the river and, therefore, in Norton.

Appropriately for a developing resort, Scarborough received an impressive station, shown on the right. The impressive facade looked on to elegant Westborough through iron railings and was constructed of ashlar stone with pavilions at each end as well as in the middle. The flamboyantly styled clock tower was added in 1884. The large Pavilion Hotel beyond the station was demolished in 1971.

Interior of Scarborough Station.

Scott Series. No 725

The interior has undergone many changes. This view shows the original double-vee overall roof. The entry from Westborough, via the station forecourt and booking hall, was on the left. Also located at this side were various waiting rooms, toilets, offices and the inevitable bookstall. Both these views of the station date from 1904-5.

To suggest ignorance of Scarborough would be verging on the improbable, for who has not heard of it, read of it, and who indeed has not been to this ever fascinating spot?

Turn wherever one will from these beautiful cliffs which converge in a castle-crowned promontory, there are gardens that feast the eye with colour and enrich the air with fragrance. Take a stance by the old castle, and view first south, then north. On either side the graceful curve of bay: sands dotted with castle builders, paddlers, bathers, donkey riders and the like. There are numerous boats in both the bays, and entering the harbour below, so much in keeping with its "old town" surroundings, are picturesque brown-sailed fishing craft. South or north there is ample explanation of the position Scarborough has won itself as "Queen of Watering Places." Below is the Marine Drive, that defies the wildest onslaught, and connects the north with the south side, and which has lengthened Scarborough's sea front so considerably.

Scarborough is the hub of the Yorkshire Coast, a place which all endeavour to visit, in whatever part of Yorkshire they may be staying. The hub of Scarborough is its Spa, now almost historic, and where the band is always an excellent one, and where there is the alternative of the Spa Theatre. An evening on the Spa Promenade is an evening to be remembered. Everywhere are to be seen smartly dressed people enjoying Scarborough at its best.

But the feature of Scarborough that above everything strikes the observant, is the ease with which she caters for people with tastes anything but uniform. So you find the day excursionist on the south sands, the middle class on the northern side, and the fashionable element looking down from the esplanade.

Scarborough may be said to be everything to everybody, and as if all these charms were not enough , Scarborough is singularly fortunate in being near to lovely woodland and moorland scenery. Walks, short train journeys and drives (including a series of motor charabanc runs) form no small portion of the day's programme for many visitors. Hackness, Forge Valley and Thornton Dale are among the places visited.

from 'England's Playground' published by the NER, circa 1910.

ROBINSON'S 'ROYAL BLUE' MOTOR TOURS

Starting Place and Booking Office, THE RAILWAY STATION.

J Robinson & Son were well known in Scarborough from the turn of the century as cab and charabanc proprietors. Their fleet included horse drawn as well as motor vehicles. They advertised 1/- cab fares from all parts of Scarborough to the station, with accompanied luggage carried free. The firm eventually owned a fleet of about twenty motor charabancs, including Lancias and Maudslays. Robinson's eventually took over tours from the station.

In the station forecourt awaiting departure on an excursion, this typical Robinson charabanc was of later vintage than the NER Saurers on the front cover, but had solid tyres and a 12mph speed limit. A local photographer was usually on hand to record the start of tours, in the hope of selling prints to some of the trippers on the return from their tour.

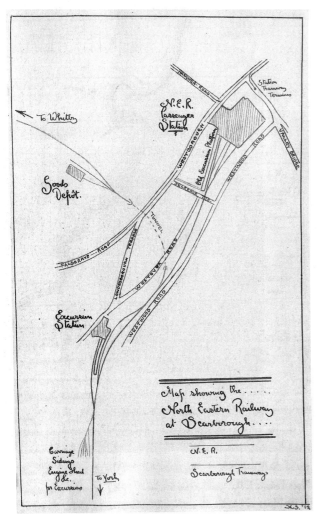

Map showing the......
North Eastern Railway
at Scarborough....

N. E. R.

Scarborough Tramways

Scarborough had a separate excursion station from 1908 until 1963. It was known as Londesborough Road from 1933 onwards. Harold Smith penned its praises in June 1912:

We ran into Scarborough Excursion Station at twenty to ten. The words "Excursion Station" usually conjure up a mental picture of a bare wooden platform, devoid of shelter, inconvenient and awkward of access. Such are the excursion stations at Blackpool and Southport. But they do things differently on the NER. The excursion station at Scarborough IS an excursion station; convenient, comfortable and specially suited to the needs of excursionists.

The platform is very broad and substantially built of stone and gravel. There is a big covered circulating area, capable of dealing with the biggest bank holiday crowd, and a cloakroom, a refreshment room and ample and commodious offices. After a dusty journey, one may have a cup of coffee, a wash and brush up in ease and comfort, and leave one's raincoat or umbrella before setting out for a day's pleasure. What other line caters as well for the day tripper? I have drawn a map showing the position of the stations in Scarborough. The Whitby line has to be worked in a rather peculiar manner owing to its position. Trains leaving Scarborough run past the end of the tunnel and then reverse, the engine being uncoupled and taken to the other end of the train, a manoeuvre which excites some astonishment in strangers.

The map, originally drawn in colour, is reproduced here.

SNAINTON . SO. YORKS

W.Hoyer

The six intermediate stations on the Forge Valley line, including Snainton, were to a uniform design in brick. Snainton, photographed here in 1905, was at the midpoint of the line and was the only station with a passing loop on this single track branch. The branch took its name from the idyllic $1^{1}/_{2}$ mile long tree-draped Forge Valley, formed by the River Derwent, and bedecked with shimmering primroses in spring and mouth-watering blackberries in late summer. Its nearest station on the line was at West Ayton, but it was named Forge Valley Station. The line was closed in 1950.

Ebberston Railway Station.

Ebberston Station, like the others on the Forge Valley line, opened in 1882 and was 2½ miles west of Snainton. Apart from the creepers, it was identical in design to Snainton. What may appear to be a complex but appealing configuration of buildings is basically a double storey house with end pavilions and annexes, the whole being brought together by a veranda. This view dates from about 1912.

18

Cayton Station was opened in 1846 on the Y&NM line to Hull and closed in 1952. The house-style features of the early station building, in this instance facing the track, were accentuated by the garden. The squat signal box was well sited for viewing each direction and controlling a level crossing. The station, seen here in 1904, served the village as well as Cayton Bay, a popular picnic spot.

Along the Coast

Two coastal lines to the north of Scarborough ran through areas of outstanding natural beauty. They were lifelines to the inhabitants of remote villages and hamlets but became popular with tourists. From his carriage window, the rail excursionist could view the sea on one side and wild moors on the other. When people turned increasingly towards their cars, the future of the lines became bleak.

The Scarborough & Whitby Railway, mainly single track, was opened in 1885. Its 21 miles took thirteen years to build. The line terminated at Whitby Town Station. The North Eastern Railway, having worked the line from the outset, absorbed it in 1898. Under the Beeching economies, it closed in March 1965.

The ambitiously titled Whitby, Redcar & Middlesbrough Union Railway, mostly single track, had to be completed by the NER after financial problems arose. Sixteen miles long, it ran from Whitby West Cliff Station to Loftus and opened in 1883. A few ironstone mines generated traffic for the line. Because of tunnels, viaducts and a generally inhospitable, if beautiful, terrain, it proved expensive to maintain and was closed in May 1958. Loftus Station, with its end on junction with a former NER line, survived a few years longer.

Photographed in 1905, Scalby Station on the Scarborough & Whitby Railway closed sixty years later. The tallest station building was the stationmaster's house. The platform seats harmonised well with the station and its horticultural trimmings. The goods yard was on the left.

Cloughton Station was similar to Scalby although the stationmaster's house was at the opposite end of the block. This had a kitchen, scullery and living room (with bay window) on the ground floor with three bedrooms and a bathroom on the first floor. Beyond the house was a ladies room, general waiting room and a booking office which also served as the stationmaster's office. The signal box controlled the level crossing. The goods yard was to the left. A 1904 view

Robin Hood's Bay Station was the largest intermediate station on the Scarborough-Whitby line. From left to right in this 1904 picture the buildings are: part of the goods warehouse, the gentlemen's toilets (behind the station sign), the booking hall (with bay window), general waiting room, ladies room and house complex. The tank provided water for the locomotives. From the station a steep twisting street led to the sea where, according to a contemporary NER guide book, "old sea captains walk back and forth as they once did on their quarter-decks, living their lives over again for the benefit of whosoever will listen."

Whitby West Cliff Station on the Whitby, Redcar & Middlesbrough Union Railway was convenient for the Spa, sands and many of the hotels and guest houses. This circa 1908 view from the south shows the main buildings on the east side, with the stationmaster's house at the far end. The goods yard was just behind the signal box on the far right. The station opened in 1883 and closed in 1961.

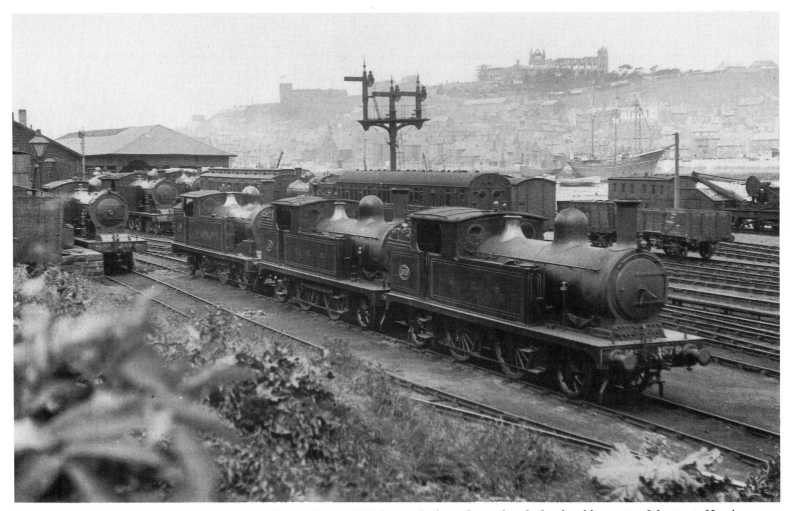

Whitby Town Station was opened in 1847 by the Whitby & Pickering Railway. It was handy for the older parts of the town. Nearby were the engine shed, goods warehouse and sidings where coal, fish and timber were handled (seen here in NER days). At this side of the signals is an autocar combination which consisted of a coupled engine and carriage. This could be driven from either the footplate or coach, depending on which was leading, hence the porthole windows on the coach.

"D.P"-596-13 SANDSEND NESS.

Opened in 1883 as part of the WR&MUR and closed in 1958, this view of Sandsend Station dates from 1925. The single track traversed the part stone and part metal viaduct before reaching the station on the left and curving round towards Sandsend Ness. Although coal traffic was handled at the station, most other goods facilities were provided at East Row, 1/2 mile nearer Whitby.

HINDERWELL

The main buildings at Hinderwell were similar to those at Sandsend and were constructed in brick. The two storey station house dominated the centre. Overall, the configuration resembled that of the Forge Valley stations except that the bay windows were absent. The second platform (nearest the camera) was added in 1908, a year before this picture was taken. Hinderwell Station served both Hinderwell and picturesque Runswick Bay just over a mile away.

The Moors

The first railway wholly within the North Riding was the Whitby & Pickering which was designed by George Stephenson and opened throughout on 26th May 1836. Horse power was used to haul the wagons and coaches over its 24 miles. The wagon bodies were constructed of wood, with sheet iron floors and sides which were removable for loading and unloading. The coaches, some with open tops, were adaptations of stagecoach bodies and on busy days, as many passengers as possible were allowed to clamber on top.

The W&PR was purchased by the York & North Midland Railway in 1845 and a limited steam hauled service was introduced in 1847. A full steam service between Whitby and Pickering was introduced by the North Eastern Railway in 1865 but only after the notorious rope-worked incline at Goathland had been bypassed. The NER's sights were set on the potential traffic to and from the industrial West Riding.

With changing needs and attitudes, the Beeching axe closed the 18 mile stretch from Grosmont to Pickering on 6th March 1965. After eight years, the line was re-opened by the North Yorkshire Moors Railway on 22nd April 1973. This preserved railway runs through the spectacular North Yorkshire Moors National Park.

The North Yorkshire & Cleveland Railway, popularly known as the Esk Valley Line, was built in sections from Picton to Grosmont during 1857-65. It was absorbed by the NER in 1859. The potential ironstone traffic to Middlesbrough and Stockton was one of the main reasons for the construction of this line. Stockton could be reached from Picton and, eventually, Middlesbrough could be reached from Battersby. The section from Middlesbrough to Whitby is still open.

North of Pickering, where the Whitby & Pickering Railway followed the Pickering Beck through Newtondale, this stern looking station building was built. Levisham Station was 1½ miles and three hundred feet below the village it served. It opened circa 1847 and was closed in 1965. The stationmaster proudly posed in front of his house and station for this 1910 photograph on a platform graced with typical NER seats and lamps.

Sleights Station was opened circa 1847 by the Y&NM after it had absorbed the Whitby & Pickering Railway. The quite elaborate GT Andrews design was reminiscent of a large dwelling house. The stone building featured mullioned windows, Tudor arches over the doors and fancy bargeboards over the roof gables. The open door led to the booking office and an advert for the Scarborough Flower Show has been strategically positioned beside it. A 1908-9 view.

At Ruswarp Station, GT Andrews used a similar design to that at Sleights but introduced Tudor arches to the windows. The chimneys also had a hint of Tudor design.

This all-embracing picture of Goathland Station shows how a country passenger station could be part of a larger configuration. Whinstone was quarried on the moors and brought by tramway to the crushing and loading plant which is partly visible on the right in this 1905 photograph. In the sidings behind the water tank are trucks laden with stone. Built by the NER in 1865 and closed by British Railways a century later, the line was to remain closed for eight years before it re-opened as a preserved line.

Goathland Station, pictured here in 1907, was largely the work of Thomas Prosser. The main station buildings, in stone, were given a rather Scottish look by the addition of crow stepped gables. Visible at the end of the platform is a water crane.

Photographed on 4th August 1973, a few months after the line was re-opened by the North Yorkshire Moors Railway as a pre-served railway, a passenger train from Grosmont was captured ascending the 1:49 gradient into Goathland Station.

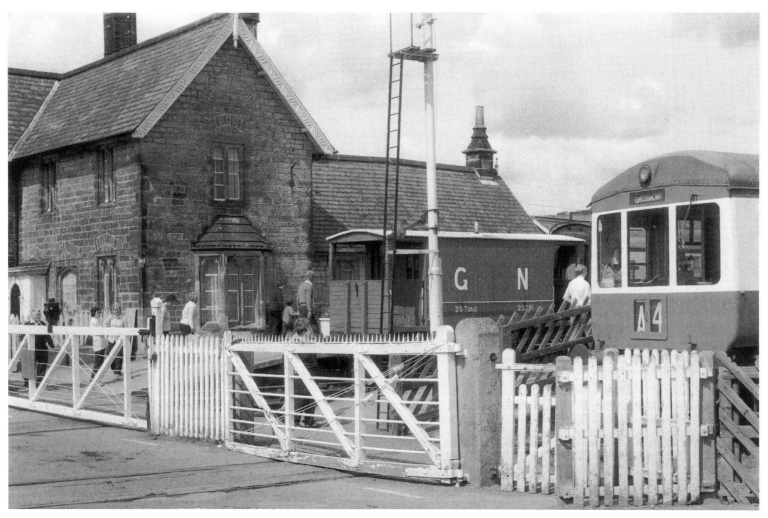

The Whitby & Pickering Railway's station at Grosmont closed in 1965. The main station building, also by Andrews, incorporated some of the features of Ruswarp and Sleights. The NYMR stock in this 1973 view shows a Great Northern Railway interloper. At Grosmont, the W&PR was joined by the Esk Valley Line, whose station (not shown) was on the other arm of the V junction.

A week before Easter 1909, Harold Smith of Bradford travelled to Whitby via Pickering on business, accompanied by his cousin. This extract comes from his record of that journey.

From Pickering to Whitby, the railway is the most windingly wild and primitively picturesque stretch of line that I ever travelled over. For the whole of those 24 miles, the railway winds through the wildest and loveliest dales in North Yorkshire. Like a sinuous serpent, the track winds in and out, no part of it in a straight line; if you were to dodge from one side of the carriage to the other, you might keep the engine in view for the whole distance. As a piece of engineering, the line is wonderful.

Leaving Pickering, the line follows the valley of Pickering Beck, gradually climbing higher and higher. Great masses of firs, pines and ash trees sweep down from the heights to the lineside. And as our little tank engine slowly puffed and snorted up the stiff grades, we simply yearned to get out and pluck the primroses and forget-me-nots which lay in glorious patches of blue and gold on the grassy banks by the stone-strewn bed of the stream. Never have I seen so many primroses!

Leaving Levisham Station, the scenery becomes wilder and more stern. The trees thin down into scattered clumps and finally give place to wild stony moorland. Through bracken and heather and hawthorn bushes, up mountainous grades (1:80 to 1:50) the line climbs up to Summit Cabin, 550 feet above sea level.

You can imagine how steep the grade is down to Whitby, for Summit Cabin is scarcely twelve miles away. We rattled down in company with the Ellerbeck, here a tiny moorland stream, crossing the Beck six times before it joins the Esk at Grosmont. At Beck Hole, the railway runs sheer on the edge of a 100 feet precipice, an awesome drop. From Grosmont, we wound along by the pleasant and smiling Esk and, passing under the imposing brick viaduct which carries the Scarborough-Saltburn line across the valley, we drew up in Whitby Town Station at twenty minutes to four.

There are two stations at Whitby: the Town Station which is a terminus, and the West Cliff Station on the Saltburn to Scarborough line. Connecting the two is a bit of line whose gradients are rather startling. As a rule, a short train of four carriages and an engine sets off from the Town Station to meet the trains at West Cliff, afterwards returning with the passengers for the Town. Some of the Saltburn trains, however, run right down into the town.

We left the station and, by a devious route, climbed to the West Cliff. Later, from the top of the cliff, we feasted our eyes on the open sea, shimmering with a silver sheen in the summer sunlight.

Danby, Lealholm, Glaisdale and Egton Stations, which were the last four constructed by the NER on the Esk Valley Line, had similar features. They all incorporated the stepped gable ends on the main and some of the ancillary buildings. This view of Lealholm Station was photographed in 1910.

Danby Station.

2416

The similarity between Danby and Lealholm (previous page) is obvious. The large stone blocks used in construction, plus the stepped gables, briefly so beloved by the NER, gave an impression of rugged indestructibility. At Danby, the effect was rather spoiled by a brick chimney stack, probably an addition, and a makeshift looking platform. Both stations were opened in 1865.

North of York

Railways of varying importance, which traversed the areas to the west and south of the North Yorkshire Moors, included part of the East Coast route between London and Edinburgh, via York and Darlington.

Passing through the Vale of York, the main line from York to Darlington was opened in 1841 by the Great North of England Railway, which became part of the North Eastern Railway. Apart from Thirsk and Northallerton, all the intermediate stations, which served largely agricultural communities, have closed. Long straight stretches of track and negligible gradients now permit speeds in excess of 100mph. The Leeds Northern Railway opened a line from Melmerby to Stockton in 1852. It bisected the York-Darlington line at Northallerton. The LNR became part of the NER.

In contrast, but branching from the above main line, was the independent Easingwold Railway. It was single track with no intermediate stations and was 2½ miles long. The passenger service to Easingwold lasted until 1948 with goods being carried until final closure in 1957.

Predominantly single track and firmly rural in character, the Thirsk & Malton Railway ran from Malton to Pilmoor (south of Thirsk). It opened in 1853, becoming part of the NER in the following year. The Malton-Gilling section lost its regular passenger service at the end of 1930 with the remaining section losing its service in the 1950s. Most of the stations remained open for freight traffic until the 1960s. A single track branch from Gilling to Pickering was built by the NER during 1871-75. Regular passenger services on this branch ceased in 1953.

Tollerton Station circa 1908. The station at Tollerton opened in 1841 and was rebuilt in 1899. Due to various track widening schemes, several stations on the NER main line between York and Darlington, including Tollerton, lost their original buildings. The modest new structure shown here looked incompatible with the spacious wide layout. As well as passengers, the station handled hay, potatoes and livestock.

Photographed in 1908, Alne Station on the Great North of England Railway opened in 1841 and was closed in 1958. The station building, left, which resembled a dwelling house, contrasted with the wooden structure opposite. The larger central arch of the road bridge accommodated fast trains. The right hand arch gave access to the Easingwold Railway platform.

On the Northallerton to Stockton line of the Leeds Northern Railway, Brompton Station (opened circa 1854) served the large village of the same name. Brompton was noted for its linen mills. The station building and the signal cabin were constructed in brick. Brompton was closed in 1965.

EASINGWOLD STATION.

17

The Easingwold Railway ran from Alne to the small agricultural town of Easingwold. On opening day, 25th July 1891, the children of Easingwold were allowed free rides to Alne Junction and back. The grandiose Station Hotel, left, which was not railway-owned, makes the timber passenger station building look rather inferior. The station complex, pictured here in 1905, included goods sidings, coal drops and a weigh office.

This view features Locomotive No.2, made by Hudswell Clarke of Leeds in 1903. The coaches were purchased from the North London Railway, probably in 1903 also. The coaching stock included a guard and luggage van which had a raised lookout at one end. Easingwold lost its railway line in 1948.

SLINGSBY STATION

The intermediate stations on the Thirsk & Malton Railway, which stretched from Malton to Pilmoor, included Slingsby, shown above. This view comes from a postcard sent from Slingsby to Gainsborough on 9th September 1905 by Gertie, who wrote "Arrived safely at Slingsby at 11.20."

In the middle distance, a large three storey grain warehouse, erected about 1858, is visible. The railway opened in 1853.

THE STATION HOUSE SLINGSBY.

Slingsby Station circa 1905. This exterior view of the stone-built station building shows how some early stations resembled houses. Over the level crossing, a long country lane led to picturesque Ryedale. The annexe building on the left, clearly an addition, included waiting facilities. To the right were various goods warehouses and loading docks. The picture includes the station-master, his black Labrador and the village postman. The station closed in 1931.

Coxwold Station

15

Opened in 1853 and closed exactly one hundred years later, Coxwold Station, also on the Malton-Pilmoor line, was situated in a tourist area and picturesquely sited in a shallow cutting. This view, from circa 1905, was taken a few years after the track at the station had been doubled by the addition of a passing loop. At the same time another platform was added. The station house included a first class waiting room. Beyond that building was a coal depot. The ornate building on the right served as a general waiting room. The NER's best kept station competition was repeatedly won by Coxwold. Some of the garden stone was appropriated from the ruins of Byland Abbey.

HUSTWAITE STATION

Husthwaite Gate Station, on the Malton-Pilmoor line, had an unusual layout. The 1896 extension to the stationmaster's house is discernible on the left. The points and signals were controlled from the podium near the crossing. The station itself, with its platform and timber buildings, was situated beyond. Half a mile along the road was the village of Husthwaite (population 403). A 1904 view.

A mid 1920s view of the station at Sinnington. By 1875, when this NER station opened, some distinct architectural styles were beginning to evolve. From left to right there was a booking hall, waiting area with veranda and the stationmaster's house. York Races could be reached via Coxwold.

South and West of York

Railway lines radiated from York in all directions. Those which ran south and south-west provided connections into the West Riding's industrial conurbation, now apportioned to West and South Yorkshire.

During 1839-40, a line from York to Altofts was opened by the York & North Midland Railway (which was amalgamated into the NER in 1854). The section of the East Coast Main Line which connected York and Doncaster, via Selby, was opened by the NER in 1871.

Selby, due south of York, also had important east to west rail links, all of which eventually came under the ownership of the NER. In addition, the independent Cawood, Wistow & Selby Light Railway started from Brayton Gates, west of Selby, and continued along five miles of single track to Wistow. After absorption by the NER in 1900, trains were run into Selby.

The Y&NM constructed a line between Church Fenton and Harrogate, via Tadcaster and Wetherby, in 1847-8. Until Harrogate acquired a centrally sited station, it relied on Brunswick Station (on the Stray) or Starbeck Station (a 1^1/$_2$ mile treck). The Harrogate-York line, via Knaresborough, was the culmination of several separate projects. The longest section, from York to Knaresborough, was opened by the East & West Yorkshire Junction Railway in 1848. The present Harrogate Station dates from 1862. It brought a number of rail services into the spa town, all of which were eventually controlled by the NER.

Until 1967, it was possible to travel north from Harrogate by the old Leeds & Thirsk Railway (it later became the Leeds Northern Railway) which connected with Ripon, Thirsk and Northallerton.

Selby, with its magnificent Abbey, also achieved fame as a rope making, trawler building and oil milling centre. The 1840 Leeds & Selby Railway station replaced an earlier, smaller one further east. It was much altered and expanded towards the end of the 19th Century. The wide canopies, with decorative valances, added a touch of luxury to an otherwise architecturally restrained station.

CAWOOD STATION

The Cawood, Wistow and Selby Light Railway line to Cawood attracted appreciable amounts of passenger and goods business, particularly in its early days. When this picture was taken in 1906 there were five return workings per day in each direction as well as freight trains carrying potatoes, sugar beet, hay and clover. The main station buildings are hidden behind the coaches. The line opened in 1898 and closed in 1930.

BOLTON PERCY

BOLTON PERCY STATION

In conjunction with track widening on the former York & North Midland line from York to Altofts, Bolton Percy Station was rebuilt to the form shown here in 1904. An island platform, new station buildings and a substantial ramp from the road bridge were constructed. Bolton Percy was opened in 1839 and survived until 1965.

From the Thomas Prosser era, the brick-built Escrick Station, between York and Selby, had style and elegance, augmented by the floral displays around the bay windows. Behind the farthest bay was a room for first class passengers. Having obtained a ticket, access to the other platform was via the road bridge. A notice beside the steps instructed the passengers to go that way. The station opened in 1871 by the NER and lasted until 1953.

Photographed about 1904, Tadcaster Station had some ecclesiastical style stone buildings. On the right can be seen an ornamental bay window and the arched doorway to the booking office. Nearby, on the trolley, are various items of travel impedimenta. The platforms had an overall roof, or trainshed. With several breweries in the town, the station sidings did brisk business in ale casks. Tadcaster was opened by the York and North Midland Railway in 1847 and closure was in 1964.

Spofforth Station was the only station on the York & North Midland between Wetherby and Harrogate. In cottage style, with quoin work at the corners, the buildings were the work of GT Andrews and, when this photograph was taken in 1912, were complemented by cottage flowers. Spofforth Station was opened in 1847 and closed in 1964.

The 1862 long low principal station building at Harrogate, which acted as a facade, was partially obscured by the later concourse and glazed over cab stand. In the 1960s and after, the station was further extensively altered. Station Square, here looking austere but agreeable, has undergone many changes. A 1915 view.

The North Eastern's Knaresborough Station was opened in 1851 and rebuilt in 1865. This photograph, from 1971, illustrates how any harshness in the station's brickwork and canopy were reduced by careful use of arches and curves. The track in the distance, beyond the crossing, traversed the famous viaduct over the river.

STATION STARBECK.

Rebuilt in 1898, fifty years after opening, Starbeck Station was graced with pitched-style awnings. They can be clearly seen in this 1908 view and extended over the largely timber buildings on each platform. They were joined by cross-members with pierced quatrefoils. The station has now lost these structures.

This view of Cattal Station, opened by the East & West Yorkshire Junction Railway in 1848, dates from 1905. The station, between Knaresborough and York, looks delightful in this view, with architecturally pleasing buildings and the adjacent Victoria Inn. The small hut near the crossing contained the signal levers. This was later replaced by a proper signal box. When the station was deprived of its awning some years ago it lost much of its character.

Situated north of Harrogate on the now defunct NER line to Ripon, the station, pictured here in 1905, served the hamlet of Wormald Green as well as the village of Markington, a mile away. The double storey station house is almost obscured by the rather austere station buildings, on which advertising material seems to have been used to relieve the architectural paucity. Opened in 1848, the station was subsequently rebuilt around 1865 and closed in 1962.

The Dales

The Yorkshire Dales, on the opposite side of the Plain of York to the North Yorkshire Moors, were favourably served by railways, most of which came under the aegis of the North Eastern Railway. Rivers flowed down each dale in a generally east or south-easterly direction. The valley contours proved advantageous when the railways were engineered. Workaday freight traffic and weekend tourist traffic were not enough, however, to guarantee the ultimate survival of the lines.

Arguably the most interesting lines were on the route up Nidderdale. The NER branch from Ripley Junction to Pateley Bridge was opened in 1862 and closed to passengers in 1951. Bradford Corporation assumed responsibility for constructing the standard gauge (4ft 8½ in) Nidd Valley Light Railway from Pateley Bridge to Lofthouse, with an extension to Angram, where its reservoir was under construction. The latter replaced a contractor's 3ft gauge line to the reservoir site.

The short NER branch to Masham, which opened in 1875, started from the main line at Melmerby and ran close to the River Ure at Tanfield and Masham. Passenger services ceased in 1931. The real Wensleydale branch only followed the Ure above Leyburn. It left the main line at Northallerton and was constructed in stages between 1848 and 1878. The various companies involved were absorbed by the NER, which built the last section from Leyburn to Hawes in 1877-8. Regular passenger services ceased in 1954.

From Eryholme Junction, south of Darlington, a branch, initiated by the Great North of England Railway, reached Swaledale at Catterick Bridge and ran parallel with the River Swale up to Richmond. It opened in 1846, passed to the NER in 1854 and closed to passengers in 1969.

DARLEY STATION

The single platform at Darley Station, on the NER's Nidderdale branch, had quite a spread of buildings. Travellers could reach the station by negotiating the wooden stile, climbing a short ramp with a handrail and crossing the track. There were no fast expresses! The station opened in 1864 and this view dates from 1908. Closure was in 1951.

DACRE STATION.

DACRE

Photographed circa 1908, Dacre Station, also on the Nidderdale branch, served the village of Dacre Banks. The station was originally also known as Dacre Banks and opened in 1862. This photograph epitomises the country station with the milk churns adding the finishing touch. Unlike Darley, this station incorporated the esteemed NER stepped gable ends. Closure was in 1951.

From six or seven trains per weekday in each direction at the turn of this century, the Nidderdale service had fallen back to only four or five trains in 1932. The service declined further before closure. All passenger trains started or terminated at Harrogate and Dacre was the busiest intermediate station. Dacre also served Summerbridge, half a mile distant. With passenger and freight handling, including timber, the large contingent of NER staff, shown posed on the platform in 1914, was perhaps justified.

The principal station building at Pateley Bridge had stepped gable ends. Any harshness was relieved by the simple, but elegant, canopy which extended along the platform, and the use of shrubs, plants and creepers. The station was opened by the NER in 1862. Although passenger services ceased in 1951, freight traffic continued until 1964.

Pateley Bridge received another station when this one, on the Nidd Valley Light Railway, was opened in 1907. It was a quarter of a mile northwest of its NER counterpart. The stations were linked but through services were rare. The second-hand coaching stock on the right was purchased from the Metropolitan Railway. The Nidd Valley Light Railway and Pateley Bridge's second station were closed in 1930.

The four stations on the Nidd Valley Light Railway, including Ramsgill above, acquired matching stone buildings, with living accommodation on the first floor for the stationmaster and his family. The building at Pateley Bridge faced down the platform. Apart from the small awnings, the structures showed, unusually for 1907, a return to the house style. Each station possessed a goods shed. Pateley Bridge also had a signal box, while the other stations had an outside lever frame like the one shown above.

STATION LOFTHOUSE 56

The above steam railcar was bought by Bradford Corporation in 1921 from the Great Western Railway and put in service on the NVLR. Passenger services terminated at Lofthouse, but freight and workmen were conveyed on an extension to Angram and Scar Reservoirs, which were completed in 1919 and 1936 respectively. The ornate platform seat and decorative work on the edge of the awning are worthy of note. This view dates from either 1921 or 1922.

The contractors for Angram Reservoir, John Best & Sons, Ltd. of Edinburgh, constructed a three foot gauge light railway from Lofthouse to the reservoir site. It was changed to standard gauge during 1906-7 and used as an extension to the NVLR. There were no stations on this part of the line but passengers were occasionally carried and a simple platform was constructed at the reservoir contractor's village at Angram. This 3 ft gauge locomotive was named after this village and the photograph dates from 1904. It is hauling a liquid supply train some miles below the village. Was it beer for the navvies?

The station buildings at Masham (opened 1875) were probably designed by Thomas Prosser in what was to become known as the NER villa-type design. Similar designs were to be found along the Wensleydale branch. The station handled goods traffic until late in 1963, almost thirty three years after its closure to passengers.

Masham Station was inconveniently situated a mile from the small town it served. The station and goods yard, each of which extended some distance to the right, were here photographed circa 1906 from the rough approach road. The buildings facing the station yard are shown from the opposite side on the previous page. Large quantities of coal were handled in the goods yard.

Bedale Station was on the stretch of line opened by the Bedale & Leyburn Railway in 1855-6 and later extended up Wensleydale by the NER. Although the station is shown deserted, it served an active market town. A partly-enclosed single storey waiting area was appended to the station house. NER type seats, scales, a vending machine and several barrows and trolleys feature in this 1904-5 view. In the distance are sidings, a level crossing and a signal box. This station closed in 1954.

At its opening in 1854, Jervaulx Station was known as Newton-le-Willows Station as it was located in the village of that name. To prevent confusion with an identically-named Lancashire town's station, it was renamed after Jervaulx Abbey in 1877. The abbey was over four miles away! Main embellishments on the simple station buildings were the stepped gables. Was Jervaulx Station the inspiration for the NER's subsequent use of this feature?

The four intermediate stations on the NER-constructed part of the Wensleydale branch (Wensley, Redmire, Aysgarth and Askrigg) were markedly similar. This is partly evident when comparing Aysgarth on this page with Askrigg on the next. At Aysgarth, from left to right, were the booking office, waiting area and stationmaster's house. The waiting room was behind the waiting area. The bay window allowed station staff to view train arrivals and passenger activity, a lot of which is evident here. Opened in 1878, the Wensleydale branch closed in 1954. Was this 1908-9 party bound for the famous falls?

30973 Askrigg. C.N.

The station, to the villa-type design, is pictured along with the commodious station yard and the village of Askrigg on the nearby hillside. Askrigg and Redmire Stations had a single platform, but Aysgarth and Wensley had additional opposite platforms with waiting shelters.

Behind the gothic style frontage of Richmond Station, designed by GT Andrews, were the booking hall, waiting rooms, stationmaster's office, porters' room, toilets, etc. The station had an overall roof, but only one platform. Nearby buildings included goods warehouses, an engine shed, a stationmaster's house and a signal box. The station was opened in 1846 by the Great North of England Railway and closed in 1969. This view from circa 1916 shows a soldier's funeral cortege.

Skipton and Beyond

Although the North Eastern Railway managed to permeate the greater part of North Yorkshire, the Midland Railway took control of the western flank. The stations it inherited from its constituent companies were varied and, in some cases, unusual.

The Leeds & Bradford Extension Railway linked the Leeds & Bradford Railway at Leeds with the East Lancashire Railway at Colne. Running via Keighley and Skipton, it was opened during 1847-9, and absorbed by the MR in 1851.

From Skipton, the North Western Railway (sometimes known as the Little North Western) opened a line to Morecambe, with a branch from Clapham to Ingleton, during 1849-50. After being operated by the MR, the NWR became part of the Midland's empire in 1871. When the London & North Western Railway (not to be confused with the Little North Western) built the viaduct at Ingleton and opened the line over Aisgill in 1861, it theoretically gave the Midland a connection into Scotland.

Following construction by the Midland Railway of the Settle to Carlisle line, the Company, in conjunction with the Lancashire & Yorkshire Railway (whose tracks were to join the MR near Hellifield) built a large new station complex at Hellifield.

The Yorkshire Dales Railway, although worked by the Midland, stayed independent until the grouping of 1923. Nine miles long, it ran from Embsay Junction to Grassington. Plans to continue the line northwards as far as Darlington were abandoned. The Midland Railway had opened a line from Skipton to Ilkley in 1888. Although it closed to passengers in 1965, Embsay Station and a stretch of track were re-opened for steam operation by a new Yorkshire Dales Railway Company in 1979.

Cononley Station

The sturdy stone buildings of Cononley Station resembled coupled houses. Concessions towards extravagance included the shaped roof tiles and bold finials, but the platform looked uneven and basic. The signal box was to a standard Midland Railway pattern, which varied in size and minor details. It had a hipped roof, unlike the NER signal boxes which had gable ends. Cononley opened as part of the Leeds & Bradford Extension Railway in 1847 and closed in 1965. It was re-opened in 1988.

In 1876, the Midland replaced the first station at Skipton by one built slightly further north. Beneath the hipped ridge-and-furrow canopies were decorative pillars and bracketry. Although few passengers are evident in this 1905-6 picture of platform 2, the Edwardian atmosphere is amply captured through the railway staff, WH Smith bookstall, adverts, trolleys and luggage. The tall cabinet near the bookstall held destination indicators, some of which are visible on an adjacent post.

This was the first station on the Leeds & Bradford Extension Railway west of Skipton and was opened in 1849. The large angular name sign was visible from each direction. The building nearest the camera illustrates how the careful use of bricks could embellish an otherwise simple structure. This station didn't last to be axed by Beeching and closed in 1952.

Gargrave Station circa 1906. The North Western Railway, often beset by working to a budget, built many of its stations from timber and plaster in a neat Tudor style. A good example was Gargrave which was built in 1849. The fencing added a little bit of luxury.

Bell Busk Station, although bearing some resemblance to Gargrave, differed in detail. It had a double storey stationmaster's house, the veranda between the gabled buildings was longer and (although not obvious from the picture) the platforms were staggered. Bell Busk Station was used by hikers who wished to see the splendid Malham area. The station lasted one hundred and ten years and was closed in 1959.

INGLETON STATION. 538.

The Midland Railway built a new stone station at the south end of Ingleton Viaduct to replace the Little North Western one. The photographer did not point his camera at the larger main buildings on the right, but at the ancillary buildings opposite, perhaps to include the beautiful hillside. The furthermost building, in stone, was probably the oldest. The nearer brick and wooden structures were most likely added to cope with increases in tourist traffic. The station was opened in 1849 and rebuilt in 1861. Passenger traffic ceased in 1954.

INGLETON STATION. No 2

Coal was mined and stone was quarried at Ingleton, but the area's outstanding asset was the magnificent countryside. The spectacular waterfalls were provided with walkways for the paying public in 1885. At weekends and holidays, inhabitants of the industrial areas of Yorkshire and Lancashire converged on Ingleton by courtesy of the MR and other railways. The train is pictured in a bay at the MR Ingleton Station. The London & North Western railway had a station at the other end of the viaduct. There, passenger services ended in 1917.

The configuration at Hellifield Station included engine sheds and extensive sidings, from where crews worked trains over the "Long Drag" to Carlisle. Passenger facilities were located on each side of the elongated island platform, which was reached through a subway. The northeast-facing side is shown, with the engine sheds in the distance. The adverts on the right helped to hide the coaling area. Hellifield Station's ornate bracketry, including the Midland's Wyvern emblem and MR monogram, is evident. Beyond the clock was the WH Smith bookstall.

The WH Smith bookstall at Hellifield was a separate unit and, although splendidly arrayed with books and postcards, hardly did justice to the prestigious station. The first class ladies' room is visible near it. Other facilities on the platform included a booking hall, refreshment room, toilets and various staff rooms. Hellifield Station opened in 1880.

Grassington Station, pictured here in 1904, was on the Yorkshire Dales Railway. The station was a terminus and served the emerging village of Grassington. It was called Grassington & Threshfield for most of its life and was situated on the Threshfield side of the river. Its construction was largely of timber. Although the branch was closed to passengers in 1930, after a short life of only 28 years, freight was carried and passenger specials ran for many years more. The line was later cut back to serve only the quarry and limeworks at Swinden, between Cracoe and Threshfield.

A 1904 view of Rylstone Station, the only intermediate station on the Yorkshire Dales Railway. It served Rylstone and also Cracoe and Hetton. Remarkably similar to Grassington, Rylstone, however, had only one platform. As at Grassington, the stationmaster's office was in the section on the left behind the clock. The stone cladding beneath the platform is redolent of Dales dry stone walling.